THE STATE
Its Historic Role

FREEDOM PRESS groups have been publishing anarchist journals, pamphlets and books ever since 1886 when the first group, which included Kropotkin, author of this pamphlet, brought out the monthly anarchist journal *Freedom*.

To commemorate the centenary the October 1986 issue of *Freedom* was produced as an 88-page volume (twice the format of this booklet) with a two-colour cover and the title FREEDOM/A HUNDRED YEARS October 1886-October 1986 (ISBN 0 980384 35 2).

It is one of FREEDOM PRESS' growing list of titles on anarchism and the anarchist approach to the major topics of our time. As well as publishing *Freedom* monthly, FREEDOM PRESS celebrated its centenary with the publication of a new 96-page anarchist quarterly *The Raven*.

The Centenary is also being marked by the publication of five volumes of selections from our journals — *Freedom, Spain and the World,* *War Commentary, Anarchy* and *Freedom* (2nd series). Our current list of publications and specimen copies of *Freedom* will be gladly sent on request (stamps to cover please).

FREEDOM PRESS
Angel Alley
84b Whitechapel High Street
London E1 7QX.

FREEDOM PRESS
Angel Alley
84b Whitechapel High Street
London E1 7QX.

Peter Kropotkin

THE STATE
Its Historic Role

A New Translation
from the French Original

FREEDOM PRESS
London
1987

Translated from the French
L'Etat — Son Role Historique (1897)

Published by
FREEDOM PRESS
In Angel Alley
84b Whitechapel High Street
London E1 7QX
1987

© English Translation by
Vernon Richards & Freedom Press
1969, 1987

ISBN 0 90384 33 6

The first English translation of
The State — Its Historic Role
appeared in serial form in the
journal FREEDOM (1897-1898) and
was reprinted as a pamphlet in 1898.
Reprinted in 1902, 1908, 1911, 1920.
Re-set and revised with an introduction
in 1943 and reprinted many times.
A new complete translation
with an introduction 1969.
Reprinted 1977.
Revised and reset with a new introduction 1987.

Printed in Great Britain by ALDGATE PRESS, LONDON E1 7QX.

TRANSLATOR'S NOTES

When Kropotkin was invited by Jean Grave, editor of *Les Temps Nouveaux*, to take part in a series of lectures to be held in the Milles Colonnes Hall in Paris in March 1896, he chose two subjects: *The State: Its Historic Role* and *Anarchism: Its Philosophy and Its Ideal*. Bearing in mind that his greatest work, *Mutual Aid*, had been appearing as a series of articles in *The Nineteenth Century* from 1890-1896 his choice of subjects for these lectures is not surprising. Kropotkin explains in the French edition of his *Memoirs* "The research that I carried out in the course of familiarising myself with the institutions of the barbarian period and those of the free cities of the Middle Ages, led me to carry out further interesting research on the role played by the State during the last three centuries, from the time of its last incarnation in Europe. In addition the study of institutions of mutual aid in the different periods of civilisation led me to enquire as to how the development of ideas of justice and morality came about in human society. I summarised my findings as two lectures: one on *The State and Its Historic Role*, and the other, in English, as *Justice and Morality*."

* * *

As it happens the lectures were never delivered. The day Kropotkin set off for Paris coincided with the decision by the heir to the Russian throne to visit Nice where he was to be welcomed by top representatives of the Government. At that time the Franco-Russian military alliance was close and important to France, and the French authorities could not risk demonstrations in Paris at the Kropotkin lecture which was expected to attract between 4-5000 people.

So when he disembarked from the Newhaven-Dieppe day boat Kropotkin was met by police officers who detained him. He was told that he had been expelled from France and would have to return by the first boat; in the event of any resistance he would be taken into 'administrative custody'. Apart from the fact that he did not get to Paris to deliver his lectures, the incident had its amusing side as well as confirming the esteem which he enjoyed even with his political enemies. He described the incident in more than one letter to his friends. Writing to James Guillaume in 1902— six years after the incident — in response to his old friend's request for a detailed account, he describes the way he was approached by the police superintendent.

"He introduced himself as Monsieur Merdès ('of Spanish descent' he added every time he repeated his name). He read out the telegram from Bourgeois [the French Prime Minister] which more or less said 'If Kropotkin disembarks inform him that he is expelled, and that he must return with the first boat. If he resists take him into administrative custody'.

"'Very well', I replied, 'I shall send telegrams to Grave and my wife'. Which is what I did.

"As to my return; I had come on the day service, in second class; the sea was terrible — so rough that I, who had never suffered from sea-sickness, had to lie down (I was just convalescing after a bout of influenza). Very well, I shall return tomorrow morning', I said, 'with the day boat'.

"'No', answered Monsieur Merdès of Spanish origin and many grimaces. 'You must return immediately by the night boat — or I shall have to put you in prison. Your cell is already prepared.'

"Then from one o'clock till late at night they telegraphed all over France to find out whether I could spend the night at an hotel (with two policemen in the next room) or whether I had to be taken to prison. The Deputy Prefect did not dare to take upon himself this terrible responsibility. Nor did the Prefect. They even telegraphed and telephoned to Nice.

"At ten o'clock Monsieur Merdès returned beaming: 'The Minister will allow you to spend the night in the hotel'.

"'The weather is fairly good', I said. 'So telegraph the Minister that I am returning by the night boat'. Which was what I did."

★   ★   ★

Kropotkin's brilliant, erudite, provocative lecture needs no formal introduction from a latter-day translator. And one assumes that the reader is prepared to make the necessary time adjustment and allowances for 'contemporary' references that are no longer contemporary but still interesting and relevant to our time; and for forecasts that have alas been proved over-optimistic; possibly too for Kropotkin's undue enthusiasm for an historic past the glories of which are sometimes given more emphasis than are its less attractive aspects.

Some readers may also question the value of detailed knowledge of the distant past for those who are seeking in the present, even modestly, to influence by direct action the future. For if we believe that Man makes history and not that Man is determined by history then it should be sufficient to know what one wants to change in society and that there are also enough people prepared to act to bring about those changes, for the social revolution to take place.

When the above paragraph was written for the 1969 edition I asked: "There surely must be a flaw in this argument in view of the fact that in 1969 Marxist determinism is at its lowest ebb; the State is on the one hand discredited by the Left and the Right yet on the other assumes more and more functions (good and bad) partly because it is assumed by Left and Right that it is the State's function to do so! I think there is no flaw in the classical anarchist argument as expressed by Kropotkin in the concluding sections of this lecture, and the young 'anarcho-Maoists', and their 'anarcho-Che-Guevarist' contemporaries will probably learn more from Kropotkin's interpretation of social history than from the brothers Cohn-Bendit's *Obsolete Communism* (Deutsch, London 1968), however much one welcomes with open arms the advent of 'Danny le Rouge' and his generation."

How far away May 1968 now seems politically in a 1986 when from Thatcher to Reagan, from Chirac to Kohl, Western politics is dominated by a Rightist laissez faire philosophy which exalts 'individual initiative' and decries 'State interference'; when that pillar of the State — the Church — is now in many parts of the world in open rebellion against government; and not all the Judiciary is as accommodating as at present in this country where it ignores police excesses and implements with enthusiasm the government's campaign to destroy Trades Unionism.

*   *   *

For Kropotkin "the State idea means something quite different
from the idea of government" and those who think otherwise are
"confusing" the two concepts. One eminent anarchist thinker who
did just this was Malatesta who in his essay *Anarchy*, first published
in 1891,* a few years before Kropotkin's *The State*, has this to say
on the subject:

Anarchists, including this writer, have used the word State, and
still do, to mean the sum total of the political, legislative,
judiciary, military and financial institutions through which the
management of their own affairs, the control over their personal
behaviour, the responsibility for their personal safety, are taken
away from the people and entrusted to others who, by usurpation
or delegation, are vested with the powers to make the laws for
everything and everybody, and to oblige the people to observe
them, if need be, by the use of collective force.

In this sense the word *State* means *government*, or to put it
another way, it is the impersonal, abstract expression of that state
of affairs, personified by government: and therefore the term
abolition of the State, Society without the State, etc., describe
exactly the concept which anarchists seek to express of the
destruction of all political order based on authority.

It would seem that Malatesta's definition corresponds more closely
to the contemporary situation. This writer would even venture the
opinion that effective government is no longer in the hands of the
politicians but with the multinationals, the banks, insurance
companies and pension funds (compare the power of the Chancellor
of the Exchequer juggling with a few billion in his *annual* budget
with that of the London market's *daily* turnover of 60 billion
dollars!). And what of the recent Big Bang at the Stock Exchange
and the technological explosion which pursues its ruthless path first
to dehumanising work and life and eventually to the annihilation of
humanity. We may even live to see a privatised para-military police
force controlled by this new 'State'. Perhaps...but we can only echo
Kropotkin's final words to his lecture: "the choice lies with us!".

Colchester December 1986   Vernon Richards

* *Anarchy* by E. Malatesta in a new translation (Freedom Press, 1974).

I

IN TAKING the State and its historic role as the subject for this study, I think I am satisfying a much felt need at the present time: that of examining in depth the very concept of the State, of studying its essence, its past role and the part it may be called upon to play in the future.

It is above all over the question of the State that socialists are divided. Two main currents can be discerned in the factions that exist among us which correspond to differences in temperament as well as in ways of thinking, but above all to the extent that one believes in the coming revolution.

There are those, on the one hand, who hope to achieve the social revolution through the State by preserving and even extending most of its powers to be used for the revolution. And there are those like ourselves who see the State, both in its present form, in its very essence, and in whatever guise it might appear, an obstacle to the social revolution, the greatest hindrance to the birth of a society based on equality and liberty, as well as the historic means designed to prevent this blossoming. The latter work to abolish the State and not to reform it.

It is clear that the division is a deep one. It corresponds with two divergent currents which in our time are manifest in all philosophical thought, in literature as well as in action. And if the prevailing views on the State remain as obscure as they are today, there is no doubt whatsoever that when — and we hope, soon — communist ideas are subjected to practical application in the daily life of communities, it will be on the question of the State that the most stubborn struggles will be waged.

Having so often criticised the State as it is today, it behoves one to seek the reason for its emergence, to study in depth its past role, and to compare it with institutions that it has replaced.

Let us, first of all, be agreed as to what we wish to include by the term 'the State'.

There is, of course, the German school which takes pleasure in confusing *State* with *Society*. This confusion is to be found among the best German thinkers and many of the French who cannot visualise Society without a concentration of the State; and it is for this reason that anarchists are generally upbraided for wanting to 'destroy society' and of advocating a return to 'the permanent war of each against all'.

However to argue in this way is to overlook altogether the advances made in the domain of history in the past thirty or so years; it is to overlook the fact that Man lived in Societies for thousands of years before the State had been heard of; it is to forget that so far as Europe is concerned the State is of recent origin — it barely goes back to the sixteenth century; and finally, it is to ignore that the most glorious periods in Man's history are those in which civil liberties and communal life had not yet been destroyed by the State, and in which large numbers of people lived in communes and free federations.

The State is only one of the forms assumed by society in the course of history. Why then make no distinction between what is permanent and what is accidental?

On the other hand the *State* has also been confused with *Government*. Since there can be no State without government, it has sometimes been said that what one must aim at is the absence of government and not the abolition of the State.

However, it seems to me that State and government are two concepts of a different order. The State idea means something quite different from the idea of government. It not only includes the existence of a power situated above society, but also of a *territorial concentration* as well as the concentration *in the hands of a few of many functions in the life of societies*. It implies some new relationships between members of society which did not exist before the formation of the State. A whole mechanism of legislation and of policing has to be developed in order to subject some classes to the domination of others.

This distinction, which at first sight might not be obvious, emerges especially when one studies the origins of the State.

Indeed, there is only one way of really understanding the State, and that is to study its historic development, and this is what we shall try to do.

The Roman Empire was a State in the real sense of the word. To this day it remains the legist's ideal. Its organs covered a vast domain with a tight network. Everything gravitated towards Rome: economic and military life, wealth, education, nay, even religion. From Rome came the laws, the magistrates, the legions to defend the territory, the prefects and the gods. The whole life of the Empire went back to the Senate — later to the Caesar, the all powerful, omniscient, god of the Empire. Every province, every district had its Capitol in miniature, its small portion of Roman sovereignty to govern every aspect of daily life. A single law, that imposed by Rome, dominated that Empire which did not represent a confederation of fellow-citizens but was simply a herd of *subjects*.

Even now, the legist and the authoritarian still admire the unity of that Empire, the unitarian spirit of its laws and, as they put it, the beauty and harmony of that organisation.

But the disintegration from within, hastened by the barbarian invasion; the extinction of local life, which could no longer resist the attacks from outside on the one hand nor the canker spreading from the centre on the other; the domination by the rich who had appropriated the land to themselves and the misery of those who cultivated it — all these causes reduced the Empire to a shambles, and on these ruins a new civilisation developed which is now ours.

So, if we leave aside the civilisation of antiquity, and concentrate our attention on the origin and developments of this young barbarian civilisation, right up to the times when, in its turn, it gave birth to our modern States, we will be able to capture the essence of the State better than had we directed our studies to the Roman Empire, or to that of Alexander of Macedonia, or again the despotic monarchies of the East.

In using, for instance, these powerful barbarian overthrowers of the Roman Empire as our point of departure, we will be able to retrace the evolution of our whole civilisation, from its beginnings and up to its Statal phase.

II

Most philosophers of the eighteenth century had very elementary ideas on the origin of societies.

According to them, in the beginning Mankind lived in small isolated families, and perpetual warfare between them was the normal state of affairs. But, one fine day, realising at last the disadvantages of their endless struggles, men decided to socialise. A social contract was concluded among the scattered families who willingly submitted themselves to an authority which — need I say? — became the starting-point as well as the initiator of all progress. And does one need to add, since we have been told as much at school, that our present governments have so far remained in their noble role as the salt of the earth, the pacifiers and civilisers of the human race?

This idea dominated the eighteenth century, a period in which very little was known about the origins of Man; and one must add that in the hands of the Encyclopaedists and of Rousseau, the idea of the 'social contract' became a weapon with which to fight the divine rights of kings. Nevertheless, in spite of the services it may have rendered in the past, this theory must be seen to be false.

The fact is that all animals, with the exception of some carnivores and birds of prey, and some species which are becoming extinct, live in societies. In the struggle for life, it is the gregarious species which have an advantage over those that are not. In every animal classification they are at the top of the ladder and there cannot be the slightest doubt that the first human beings with human attributes were already living in societies.

Man did not create society; society existed before Man.

We now also know — and it has been convincingly demonstrated by anthropology — that the point of departure for mankind was not the family but the clan, the tribe. The patriarchal family as we know it, or as it is depicted in Hebrew traditions, did not appear until very much later. man spent tens of thousands of years in the clan or tribal phase — let us call it the primitive tribe or, if you wish, the savage tribe — and during this time man had already developed a whole series of institutions, habits and customs much earlier than the institutions of the patriarchal family.

In these tribes, the separate family no more existed than it exists among so many other sociable mammals. Any division within the tribe was mainly between generations; and from a far distant age, going right back to the dawn of the human race, limitations had been imposed to prevent sexual relations between the different generations, which however were allowed between those of the same generation. One can still find traces of that period in some contemporary tribes as well as in the language, customs and superstitions of peoples of a much higher culture.

Hunting and food-gathering were engaged in by the whole tribe in common, and once their hunger was satisfied, they gave themselves up with passion to their dramatised dances. To this day we still find tribes who are very close to this primitive phase living on the periphery of the large continents, or in the vicinity of mountainous regions, in the least accessible parts of the world.

The accumulation of private property could not then take place there, since anything that had been the personal possession of a member of the tribe was destroyed or burned where his body was buried. This is still done, in England too, by the Gypsies, and funeral rites of 'civilised' people still bear the imprint of this custom: thus the Chinese burn paper models of the dead person's possessions, and at the military leader's funeral his horse, his sword and decorations accompany him as far as his grave. The meaning of the institution has been lost, but the form has survived.

Far from expressing contempt for human life, those primitive people hated murder and blood. To spill blood was considered such a grave matter, that every drop spilled — not only human blood but also that of some animals — required that the aggressor should lose an equal amount of his own blood.

Furthermore, murder within the tribe is something *quite unknown*; for instance among the Inuits or Eskimos — those survivors of the Stone Age who inhabit the Arctic regions — or among the Aleutians, etc., one definitely knows that there has not been a single murder *within the tribe* for fifty, sixty or more years.

But when tribes of different origin, colour and language met in the course of their migrations, it often ended in war. It is true that even then men were seeking to make these encounters more pacific. Tradition, as Maine, Post and E. Nys have so well demonstrated, was already developing the germs of what in due course became International Law. For instance, a village could not be attacked without warning the inhabitants. Never would anyone dare to kill on the path used by women to reach the spring. And often to make peace it was necessary to balance the numbers of men killed on both sides.

However, all these precautions and many others besides were not enough: solidarity did not extend beyond the confines of the clan or tribe; quarrels arose between people of different clans and tribes, which could end in violence and even murder.

From that period a general law began to be developed between the clans and tribes. 'Your members have wounded or killed one of ours; we have a right therefore to kill one of you or to inflict a similar wound on one of you', and it did not matter who, since the tribe was always responsible for the individual acts of its members. The well-known biblical verses: "Blood for blood, an eye for an eye, a tooth for a tooth, a wound for a wound, a life for a life" — but no more! as Koenigswarter put it so well — owe their origin to them. It was their concept of justice...and we have no reason to feel superior since the principle of 'a life for a life' which prevails in our codes is only one of its many survivals.

It is clear that a whole series of institutions (and many others I shall not mention) as well as a complete code of tribal morality, were already developed during this primitive phase. And this nucleus of sociable customs was kept alive by usage, custom and tradition only. There was no authority with which to impose it.

There can be no doubt that primitive society had temporary leaders. The sorcerer, the rain-maker — the learned men of that age — sought to profit from what they knew about nature in order to dominate their fellow beings. Similarly, he who could more easily memorise the proverbs and songs in which all tradition was embodied became influential. At popular festivals he would recite these proverbs and songs in which were incorporated the decisions that had been taken on such-and-such an occasion by the people's assembly in such-and-such a connection. In many a small tribe this is still done. And dating from that age, these 'educated' members sought to ensure a dominant role for themselves by communicating their knowledge only to the chosen few, to the initiates. All religions, and even the arts and all trades have begun with 'mysteries', and modern research demonstrates the important role that secret societies of the initiates play to maintain some traditional practices in primitive clans. Already the germs of authority are present there.

It goes without saying that the courageous, the daring and, above all, the prudent, also became the temporary leaders in the struggles with other tribes or during migrations. But there was no alliance between the bearer of the 'law' (the one who knew by heart the tradition and past decisions), the military chief and the sorcerer; and the *State* was no more part of these tribes than it is of the society of bees or ants, or of our contemporaries the Patagonians and the Eskimos.

Nevertheless that phase lasted for many thousands of years, and the barbarians who overran the Roman Empire had also gone through this phase and were only just emerging from it.

In the early centuries of our era there were widespread migrations of the tribes and confederations of tribes that inhabited Central and Northern Asia. Waves of small tribes driven by more or less civilised peoples who had come down from the high tablelands of Asia — they themselves had probably been driven away by the rapid desiccation of these plateaux[1] — spread all over Europe, each driving the other and being assimilated in their drive towards the West.

In the course of these migrations, in which so many tribes of different origins became assimilated, the primitive tribe which still existed among most of the savage inhabitants of Europe could not avoid disintegration. The tribe was based on a common origin and the cult of common ancestors; but to which common origin could these agglomerations of people appeal when they emerged from the confusion of migrations, drives, inter-tribal wars, during which here and there one could already observe the emergence of the

[1]The reasons which lead me to this hypothesis are put forward in a paper, *Dessication of Eur-Asia*, compiled for the Research Department of the Geographical Society of London, and published in its *Geographical Journal* for June 1904.

paternal family — the nucleus formed by the exclusive possession by some of women won or carried off from neighbouring tribes?

The old ties were broken, and to avoid disruption (which, in fact, did occur for many tribes, which disappeared for ever) new links had to be forged. And they were established through the communal possession *of the land* — of the terrory on which each agglomeration had finally settled.[2]

The possession in common of a particular area — of this small valley or those hills — became the basis for a new understanding. The ancestral gods lost all meaning; so then local gods, of that small valley or this river or that forest, gave their religious sanction to the new agglomerations by replacing the gods of the original tribe. Later Christianity, always willing to adjust to pagan survivals, made them into local saints.

Henceforth, the village community consisting entirely or partly of individual families — all united, however, by the possession in common of the land — became the essential link for centuries to come.

Over vast areas of eastern Europe, Asia and Africa it still survives. The barbarians — Scandinavians, Germans, Slavs, etc. — who destroyed the Roman Empire lived under such an organisation. And by studying the codes of the barbarians of that period, as well as the confederations of village communities that exist today among the Kabyles, the Mongols, the Hindus, the Africans, etc., it has been possible to reconstruct in its entirety that form of society which was the starting point of our present civilisation as it is today.

Let us therefore have a look at this institution.

[2]Readers interested in this subject as well as in that of the communal phases and of the free cities, will find more detailed information and source references in my book *Mutual Aid*.

III

The village community consisted then, as it still does, of individual families. But all the families of the same village owned the land in common. They considered it as their common heritage and shared it out among themselves on the basis of the size of each family — their needs and their potential. Hundreds of millions of human beings still live in this way in Eastern Europe, India, Java, etc. It is the same kind of system that has been established in our time by Russian peasants, freely in Siberia, as soon as the State gave them a chance to occupy the vast Siberian territory in their own way.

Today the cultivation of the land in a village community is carried out by each individual household independently. Since all the arable land is shared out between the families (and further shared out when necessary) each cultivates its field as best it can. But originally, the land was also worked in common, and this custom is still carried on in many places — at least on a part of the land. As to the clearing of woodland and the thinning of forests, the construction of bridges, the building of small forts and turrets, for use as places of safety in the event of invasion — all these activities were carried out on a communal basis, just as hundreds of millions of peasants still do where the village commune has held out against the encroachments of the State. But 'consumption' — to use a modern term — was already operating on a family basis, each family having its cattle, its kitchen garden and stores. The means both for hoarding and for handing down goods and chattels accumulated through inheritance had already been introduced.

In all its affairs the village commune was sovereign. Local custom was law and the plenary assembly of all the heads of family, men and women, was the judge, the only judge, in civil and criminal matters. When an inhabitant had lodged a complaint against another and stuck his knife in the ground at the place where the commune normally assembled, the commune had to 'find the sentence' according to local custom once the *fact* of an offence had been established by the juries of the two parties in litigation.

Were I to recount all the interesting aspects of this phase, I would not have the space in which to do so. I must therefore refer the

reader to *Mutual Aid*. Suffice it to mention here that *all* the
institutions which States were to seize later for the benefit of
minorities, that all notions of law that exist in our codes (which
have been mutilated in favour of minorities) and all forms of
judicial procedure, in so far as they offer guarantees to the
individual, had their beginnings in the village commune. So when
we imagine that we have made great advances in introducing, for
instance, the jury, all we have done is to return to the institution of
the so-called 'barbarians' after having changed it to the advantage of
the ruling classes. Roman law was simply grafted to customary law.

The sense of national unity was developing at the same time
through large free federations of village communes.

The village commune, being based on the possession in common
and very often in the cultivation in common of the land; and being
sovereign both as judge and legislator of customary law, satisfied
most of the needs of the social being.

But not all its needs: there were still others that had to be
satisfied. Now, the spirit of the times was not to appeal to a
government as soon as a new need was making itself felt. On the
contrary the individuals themselves would take the initiative to
come together, to join forces, and to federate; to create an entente,
large or small, numerous or restricted, which was in keeping with
the new need. And society then was literally covered, as if by a
network, of sworn brotherhoods; of guilds for mutual aid, of
'conjurations', in the village as well as outside it, in the federation.

We may observe this phase and spirit at work even today, among
many barbarian federations, which have remained outside the
modern States copied on the Roman or rather Byzantine model.

Thus, to take one example among many, the Kabyles have
maintained their village community, with the characteristics I have
just mentioned: land in common, communal tribunals, etc. But
man feels the need for action beyond the narrow confines of his
hamlet. Some rove the world seeking adventure as pedlars. Others
take up some kind of trade — or 'art'. And those pedlars and those
artisans join together in 'fraternities', even when they belong to
different villages, tribes or confederations. Union is needed for
mutual succour on voyages to distant lands, for the mutual
exchange of the mysteries of one's trade, and so they join forces.

They swear brotherhood and practise it in a way that makes a deep impression on Europeans; it is a real brotherhood and not just empty words.

Furthermore, misfortune can overtake anyone. Who knows but that tomorrow in a brawl a normally gentle and quiet man may exceed the established limits of decorum and sociability? Who knows whether he might resort to blows and inflict wounds? It will be necessary to pay heavy compensation to the offended or wounded party; it will be necessary to plead one's cause before the village assembly, and to reconstruct the facts, on the testimony of six, ten or twelve 'sworn brothers'. All the more reason to enter a fraternity.

Besides, man feels the need to meddle in politics, to engage in intrigue perhaps, or to propagate a particular moral opinion or a particular custom. Finally, external peace has to be safeguarded; alliances with other tribes to be concluded, federations to be constituted far and wide; elements of intertribal law to be spread abroad. Well then, to gratify all these needs of an emotional or intellectual nature, the Kabyles, the Mongols, the Malays, do not appeal to a government; they haven't one. Being men of customary law, and individual initiative, they have not been perverted from acting for themselves by the corrupting force of government and Church. They unite spontaneously. They form sworn brotherhoods, political and religious associations, craft associations — *guilds* as they were called in the Middle Ages, and *cofs* as they are called today by the Kabyles. And these *cofs* extend beyond the boundaries of the hamlet; they extend far and wide into the desert and to foreign cities; and brotherhood is practised in these associations. To refuse help to a member of one's *cof* — even at the risk of losing all one's possessions and one's life — is to commit an act of treason to the 'brotherhood'; it is to be treated as one's 'brother's' murderer.

What we find today among the Kabyles, Mongols, Malays, etc., was the very essence of life of the barbarians in Europe from the fifth to the twelfth and even until the fifteenth century. Under the name of *guilds, friendships, brotherhoods,* etc., associations abounded for mutual defence, to avenge affronts suffered by some members of the union and to express solidarity, to replace the 'eye for an eye' vengeance by compensation, followed by the acceptance of the aggressor in the brotherhood; for the exercise of trades, for aid in case of illness, for defence of the territory; to prevent encroachments of a nascent authority; for commerce, for the practice of 'good neighbourliness'; for propaganda — in a word for all that Europeans, educated by the Rome of the Caesars and the Popes, nowadays expect from the State. It is even very doubtful whether there was a single man in that period, free man or serf, apart from those who had been banned by their own brotherhoods, who did not belong to a brotherhood or some guild, as well as to his commune.

The Scandinavian *Sagas* extol their achievements; the devotion of sworn brothers is the theme of the most beautiful poems. Of course, the Church and nascent kings, representatives of the Byzantine (or Roman) law which reappeared, hurl their excommunications and their rules and regulations at the brotherhood, but fortunately they remained a dead letter.

The whole history of the epoch loses its meaning and is quite incomprehensible if one does not take those brotherhoods into consideration, these unions of brothers and sisters, which sprang up everywhere to deal with the many needs in the economic and personal lives of the people.

In order to appreciate the immense progress achieved by this double institution of village communities and freely sworn brotherhoods — outside any Roman Catholic or Statist influence — take for instance Europe as it was at the time of the barbarian invasion, and compare it with what it became in the tenth and eleventh centuries. The untamed forest is conquered and colonised; villages cover the country and are surrounded by fields and hedges, and protected by small forts interlinked by paths crossing the forests and the marshes.

In these villages one finds the seeds of industrial arts and discovers a whole network of institutions for maintaining internal and external peace. In the event of murder or woundings the villagers no longer seek as in the tribe, to eliminate or to inflict an equivalent wound on the aggressor, or even one of his relatives or some of his fellow villagers. Rather is it the brigand-lords who still adhere to that principle (hence their wars without end), whereas among villagers *compensation*, fixed by arbiters, becomes the rule after which peace is re-established and the aggressor is often, if not always, adopted by the family who has been wronged by his aggression.

Arbitration for all disputes becomes a deeply rooted institution in daily use — in spite of and against the bishops and the nascent kinglets who would wish every difference should be laid before them, or their agents, in order to benefit from the *fred* — the fine formerly levied by the village on violators of the peace when they brought their dispute before them, and which the kings and bishops now appropriate.

And finally hundreds of villages are already united in powerful federations, sworn to internal peace, who look upon their territory as a common heritage and are united for mutual protection. These were the seeds of European *nations*. And to this day one can still study those federations in operation among the Mongol, the Turko-Finnish and Malayan tribes.

Meanwhile black clouds are gathering on the horizon. Other unions — of dominant minorities — are also established, which seek slowly to make these free men into serfs, into subjects. Rome is dead, but its tradition is reborn, and the Christian church, haunted by the visions of Eastern theocracies, gives its powerful support to the new powers that seek to establish themselves.

Far from being the bloodthirsty beast he was made out to be in order to justify the need to dominate him, Man has always preferred peace and quiet. Quarrelsome rather than fierce, he prefers his cattle, the land, and his hut to soldiering. For this reason, no sooner had the great migrations of barbarians slowed down, no sooner had the hordes and the tribes fortified themselves more or less in their respective territories, than we see that defence of the territory against new waves of emigrants is entrusted to someone who engages a small band of adventurers — hardened warriors or brigands — to follow him, while the overwhelming majority engages in rearing cattle, in working the land. And that defender soon begins to accumulate riches; he gives horses and iron (then very expensive) to the miserable cultivator who has neither horse nor plough, and reduces him to servitude. He also begins to lay down the bases for military power.

And at the same time, little by little, the tradition that makes the law is being forgotten by the majority. In each village only a few old folk can remember the verses and songs containing the 'precedents' on which customary law is based, and on festive occasions they repeat these before the community. And slowly, certain families make it their speciality, transmitted from father to son, of remembering these songs and verses, of preserving the purity of the law. Villagers would go to them to adjudicate on complicated disputes, especially when two confederations could not agree to accept the decisions of the arbiters chosen from among themselves.

Princely and royal authority is already germinating in these families, and the more I study the institutions of that period the more do I see that customary law did much more to create that authority than did the power of the sword. Man allowed himself to be enslaved much more by his desire to 'punish' the aggressor 'according to the law' than by direct military conquest.

And gradually the first 'concentration of powers', the first mutual assurance for domination — by judge and military leader — is made against the village community. A single man assumes these two functions. He surrounds himself with armed men to carry out the judicial decisions; he fortifies himself in his turret; he accumulates for his family the riches of the time — bread, cattle, iron — and slowly imposes his domination over the peasant in the vicinity.

The learned man of the period, that is the sorceror or the priest, soon gave him his support either to share his power or, by adding force to the knowledge of customary law to his powers as a feared magician, the priest takes it over himself. From which stems the temporal authority of the bishops in the ninth, tenth and eleventh centuries.

I would need a series of lectures rather than a chapter to deal with this subject which is so full of new lessons, and to recount how free men gradually became serfs, forced to work for the lord of the manor, temporal or clerical; of how authority was built up over the villages and boroughs in a tentative, groping manner; of how the peasants leagued together, rebelled, struggled to oppose this growing domination; of how they perished in those attacks against the thick walls of the castle and against the men clad in iron defending it.

It will be enough for me to say that round about the tenth and eleventh centuries the whole of Europe appeared to be moving towards the constitution of those barbarian kingdoms, similar to the ones found today in the heart of Africa, or those of theocracies one knows about from Oriental history. This could not happen in a day; but the seeds of those petty royalties and for those petty theocracies were already there and were increasingly manifesting themselves.

Fortunately the 'barbarian' spirit — Scandinavian, Saxon, Celt, German, Slav — which for seven or eight centuries had incited men to seek the satisfaction of their needs through individual initiative and through free agreement between the brotherhoods and guilds — fortunately that spirit persisted in the villages and boroughs. The barbarians allowed themselves to be enslaved, they worked for the master, but their feeling for free action and free agreement had not yet been broken down. Their brotherhoods were more alive than ever, and the crusades had only succeeded in arousing and developing them in the West.

And so the revolution of the urban communities, resulting from the union of the village community and the sworn brotherhood of the artisans and the merchant — which had been prepared long since by the federal mood of the period — exploded in the eleventh and twelfth centuries with striking effect in Europe. It had already started in the Italian communities in the tenth century.

This revolution, which most university historians prefer to ignore, or to underestimate, saved Europe from the disaster which threatened it. It arrested the development of theocratic and despotic kingdoms in which our civilisation might well have foundered, after a few centuries of pompous splendour, just as did the civilisations of Mesopotamia, Assyria and Babylon. It opened the way for a new way of life: that of the free communes.

IV

It is easy to understand why modern historians, trained in the Roman way of thinking and seeking to associate all institutions with Rome, find it so difficult to appreciate the communalist movement that existed in the eleventh and twelfth centuries. This movement with its virile affirmation of the individual, and which succeeded in creating a society through the free federation of men, of villages and of towns, was the complete negation of the unitarian, centralising Roman outlook with which history is explained in our university curricula. Nor is it linked to any historic personality, or to any central institution.

It is a natural development, belonging, just as did the tribe and the village community, to a certain phase in human evolution, and not to any particular nation or region. This is the reason why academic science cannot be sensitive to its spirit and why the Augustin Thierrys and the Sismondis, historians who really had understood the mood of the period, have not had followers in France, where Luchaire is still the only one to have taken up — more or less — the tradition of the great historian of the Merovingian and Communalist periods. It further explains why, in England and Germany, research into this period as well as an appreciation of its motivating forces, are of very recent origin.

The commune of the Middle Ages, the free city, owes its origin on the one hand to the village community, and on the other, to those thousands of brotherhoods and guilds which were coming to life in that period independently of the territorial union. As a federation between these two kinds of unions, it was able to assert itself under the protection of its fortified ramparts and turrets.

In many regions it was a peaceful development. Elsewhere — and this applied in general to Western Europe — it was the result of a revolution. As soon as the inhabitants of a particular borough felt themselves to be sufficiently protected by their walls, they made a 'conjuration'. They mutually swore an oath to drop all pending matters concerning slander, violence or wounding, and undertook, so far as disputes that might arise in the future, never again to have recourse to any judge other than the syndics which they themselves would nominate. In every good-neighbourly or art guild, in every sworn brotherhood, it had been normal practice for a long time. In every village community, such as had been the way of life in the past, before the bishop and the petty king had managed to introduce, and later impose on it, its judge.

Now, the hamlets and parishes which made up the borough, as well as the guilds and brotherhoods which developed within it, looked upon themselves as a single *amitas*, nominated their judges and swore permanent union between all those groups.

A charter was soon drawn up and accepted. If need be, someone would be sent off to copy the charter of some neighbouring small community (we know of hundreds of such charters) and the community was set up. The bishop or the prince, who had been until then the judge in the community, and often more or less its master, could in the circumstances only recognise the *fait accompli* — or oppose the new conjuration by force of arms. Often the king — that is the prince who sought to be a cut above the other princes and whose coffers were always empty — would 'grant' the charter for ready cash. Thus he refrained from imposing *his* judge on the community, while at the same time gaining prestige in the eyes of the other feudal lords. But this was by no means the rule; hundreds of communes remained active with no other authority than their goodwill, their ramparts and their lances.

In the course of a hundred years, this movement spread in an impressively harmonious way throughout Europe — by imitation, to be sure — covering Scotland, France, the Low Countries, Scandinavia, Germany, Italy, Poland and Russia. And when we now compare the Charters and the internal organisation of all these communities we are struck by the virtual uniformity of these Charters and the organisation that grew in the shadow of these 'social contracts'. What a striking lesson for the Romanists and the Hegelians for whom servitude before the law is the only means of achieving conformity in institutions!

From the Atlantic to the middle course of the Volga, and from Norway to Sicily, Europe was being covered with such communities — some becoming populated cities such as Florence, Venice, Amiens, Nuremberg or Novgorod, others remaining struggling villages of a hundred or as few as some twenty families, but nevertheless treated as equals by their more prosperous sisters.

As organisms bubbling with life, communities obviously developed in different ways. Geographical location, the nature of external commerce, and resistance from outside to overcome all gave each community its own history. But for all of them the basic principle was the same. The same friendship (*amitas*) of the village communities and the guilds associated within the precincts whether it was Pskov in Russia and Bruges in Flanders, a village of three hundred inhabitants in Scotland or prosperous Venice with its islands, a village in the North of France or one in Poland, or even *Florence la Belle*. They all represent the same *amitas*; the same friendship of the village communes and guilds, united behind the walled precincts. Their constitution, in its general characteristics, is the same.

Generally the walls of the town grew longer and thicker as the population grew and were flanked by towers which grew taller and taller, and were each raised by this or that district, or guild, and consequently displayed individual characteristics — the town was divided into four, five or six sections or sectors, which radiated from the citadel or the cathedral towards the city ramparts. Each of these sectors was inhabited mainly by an 'art' or trade whereas the new trades — the 'young arts' — occupied the suburbs which in due course were enclosed by a new fortified wall.

The *street*, or the parish represented the territorial unit, corresponding to the earlier village community. Each street or parish had its popular assembly, its forum, its popular tribunal, its priest, its militia, its banner and often its seal, the symbol of its sovereignty. Though federated with other streets it nevertheless maintained its independence.

The professional unit which often was more or less identified with the district or with the sector, was the guild — the trade union. The latter also had its saints, its assembly, its forum and its judges. It had its funds, its landed property, its militia and its banner. It also had its seal, symbol of its *sovereignty*. In the event of war, its militia joined, assuming it was considered expedient, with the other guilds and planted its own banner alongside the large banner (*carrosse*) of the city.

Thus the city was the union of the districts, streets, parishes and

THE STATE — ITS HISTORIC ROLE

guilds, and had its plenary assembly in the grand forum, its large belfry, its elected judges and its banner to rally the militias of the guilds and districts. It dealt with other cities as sovereign, federated with whomever it wished, concluded alliances nationally or even outside the national territory. Thus the Cinque ports around Dover were federated with French and Dutch ports across the Channel; the Russian Novgorod was the ally of the Germano-Scandinavian Hansa, and so on. In its external relations each city possessed all the attributes of the modern State. From that period onwards what came to be known later as International Law was formed by free contracts and subject to sanction by public opinion in all the cities, just as later it was to be more often violated than respected by the States.

On how many occasions would a particular city, unable 'to find the sentence' in a particularly complicated case, send someone to 'seek the sentence' in a neighbouring city! How often was the prevailing spirit of that period — arbitration, rather than the judge's authority — demonstrated with two communes taking a third one as arbitrator!

The trades also acted in this way. Their commercial and craft relations extended beyond the city, and their agreements were made without taking into account nationality. And when in our ignorance we boast of our international workers' congresses, we forget that by the fifteenth century international congresses of trades and even apprentices were already being held.

Lastly, the city either defended itself against aggressors and itself waged fierce war against the feudal lords in the neighbourhood, naming each year one or two military commanders for its militias; or it accepted a 'military defender' — a prince or a duke which it selected for one year and dismissed at will. For the maintenance of his soldiers, he would be given the receipts from judicial fines; but he was forbidden to interfere in the affairs of the city.

Or if the city were too weak to free itself from its neighbours the feudal vultures, it kept as its more or less permanent military defender, the bishop, or the prince of a particular family — Guelf or Ghibelline in Italy, the Rurik family in Russia, or the Olgerds in Lithuania — but was jealously vigilant in preventing the authority of the bishop or the prince extending beyond the men encamped in the castle. They were even forbidden to enter the city without permission. To this day the King of England cannot enter the City of London without the permission of the Lord Mayor.

The economic life of the cities in the Middle Ages would deserve to be recounted in detail. The interested reader is referred to what I have written on the subject in *Mutual Aid* in which I rely on a vast body of up-to-date historic research on the subject. Here it must suffice simply to note that internal commerce was dealt with entirely by the guilds — not by individual artisans — prices being established by mutual agreement. Furthermore, at the beginning of that period external commerce was dealt with *exclusively by the city*. It was only later that it became the monopoly of the Merchants' Guild, and later still of individual merchants. Furthermore, nobody worked on Sundays, nor on Saturday afternoons (bath day). The provisioning of the principal consumer goods was always handled by the city, and this custom was preserved for corn in some Swiss towns until the midddle of the nineteenth century.

In short there is a massive and varied documentation to show that mankind has not known, either before or since, a period of relative well-being assured to everybody as existed in the cities of the Middle Ages. The present poverty, insecurity, and physical exploitation of labour were then unknown.

V

With these elements — liberty, organisation from the simple to the complex, production and exchange by the Trades (guilds), foreign trade handled by the whole city and not by individuals, and the purchase of provisions by the city for resale to the citizens at cost price — with such elements, the towns of the Middle Ages for the first two centuries of their free existences became centres of well-being for all the inhabitants, centres of wealth and culture, such as we have not seen since.

One has but to consult the documents which made it possible to compare the rates at which work was remunerated and the cost of provisions — Rogers has done this for England and a great number of German writers for Germany — to learn that the labour of an artisan and even of a simple day-labourer was paid at a rate not attained in our time, not even by the élite among workers. The account books of colleges of the University of Oxford (which cover seven centuries beginning at the twelfth) and of some English landed estates, as well as those of a large number of German and Swiss towns, are there to bear witness.

If one also considers the artistic finish and amount of decorative work the craftsman of that period put into not only the objects of art he produced, but also into the simplest of household utensils — a railing, a candlestick, a piece of pottery — one realises that he did not know what it meant to be hurried in his work, or overworked as is the case in our time; that he could forge, sculpt, weave, or embroider as only a very small number of worker-artists among us can manage nowadays.

Finally, if one runs through the list of donations made to the churches and the communal houses of the parish, the guild or the city, both in works of art — decorative panels, sculptures, wrought-iron and cast metal — and in money, one realises the degree of well-being attained by those cities; one also has an insight into the spirit of research and invention which manifested itself, and of the breath of freedom which inspired their works, the feeling of brotherly solidarity that grew up in those guilds in which men of the same trade were united, not simply for commercial and technical reasons, but by bonds of sociability and brotherhood. Was it not in fact the rule of the guild that two brothers should sit at the bedside of each sick brother — a custom which certainly required devotion in those times of contagious diseases and the plague — and to follow him as far as the grave, and then look after his widow and children?

Abject poverty, misery, uncertainty of the morrow for the majority, and the isolation of poverty, which are the characteristics of our modern cities, were quite unknown in those 'free oases, which emerged in the twelfth century amidst the feudal jungle'.

In those cities, sheltered by their conquered liberties, inspired by the spirit of free agreement and of free initiative, a whole new civilisation grew up and flourished in a way unparalleled to this day.

All modern industry comes to us from these cities. In three centuries, industries and the arts attained such perfection that our century has only been able to surpass them in speed of production, but rarely in quality, and very rarely in the intrinsic beauty of the product. All the arts we seek in vain to revive now — the beauty of a Raphael, the strength and boldness of a Michelangelo, the art and science of a Leonardo da Vinci, the poetry and language of a Dante, and not least, the architecture to which we owe the cathedrals of Laon, Rheims, Cologne, Pisa, Florence — as Victor Hugo so well put it "le peuple en fut le maçon" (they were built by the people) — the treasures of sheer beauty of Florence and Venice, the town halls of Bremen and Prague, the towers of Nuremberg and Pisa, and so on *ad infinitum*, all was the product of that age.

Do you wish to measure the progress of that civilisation at a glance? Then compare the dome of St Mark in Venice with the rustic arch of the Normans; the paintings of Raphael with the embroidery of the Bayeux Tapestries; instruments of mathematics and physics, and the clocks of Nuremberg with the hour-glasses of the preceding centuries; the rich language of a Dante with the uncouth Latin of the tenth century. A new world was born between the two!

With the exception of that other glorious period — once more of free cities — of ancient Greece, never had humanity made such a giant step forward. Never, in the space of two or three centuries, had Man undergone such far-reaching changes, nor so extended his power over the forces of Nature.

You are perhaps thinking of the civilisation and progress of our century which comes in for so much boasting? But in each of its manifestations it is only the child of the civilisation that grew up with the free communes. All the great discoveries made by modern science — the compass, the clock, the watch, printing, maritime discoveries, gunpowder, the laws of gravitation, atmospheric pressure of which the steam engine is a development, the rudiments of chemistry, the scientific method already outlined by Roger Bacon and applied in Italian universities — where do all these originate if not in the free cities, in the civilisation which was developed under the protection of communal liberties?

It will perhaps be pointed out that I am forgetting the internal conflicts, the domestic struggles, with which the history of these communes is filled, the street riots, the bitter wars waged against the lords, the insurrection of the 'young arts' against the 'old arts', the blood spilled in those struggles and in the reprisals that followed.

No, in fact I forget nothing. But like Leo and Botta — the two historians of medieval Italy — and Sismondi, Ferrari, Gino Capponi and so many others, I see that those struggles were the very guarantee of a free life in the free city. I perceive a renewal, a new impetus towards progress after each of those struggles. After having recounted in detail these struggles and conflicts, and having measured also the greatness of the progress achieved while blood was being shed in the streets, well-being assured for all the inhabitants, and civilisation renewed — Leo and Botta concluded with this idea which is so just and of which I am frequently reminded. I would like to see it engraved in the minds of every modern revolutionary: "A commune — they said — does not represent the picture of a moral whole, does not appear universal in its manner of being, as the human mind itself, *except when it has admitted conflict, opposition.*"

Yes, conflict, freely debated, without an outside force, the State, adding its immense weight to the balance in favour of one of the forces engaged in the struggle.

I believe, with these two writers, that often "more harm has been done by *imposing* peace, because one linked together opposites in seeking to create a general political order, and sacrificed individualities and small organisms, in order to absorb them in a vast colourless and lifeless whole.

It is for this reason that the communes — so long as they did not themselves seek to become States and to impose around them "submission in a vast colourless and lifeless whole" — for this reason they grew and gained a new lease of life from each struggle, and blossomed to the clatter of swords in the streets; whereas two centuries later that same civilisation collapsed in the wake of wars fathered by the States.

In the commune, the struggle was for the conquest and defence of the liberty of the individual, for the federative principle, for the right to unite and to act; whereas the States' wars had as their objective the destruction of these liberties, the submission of the individual, the annihilation of the free contract, and the uniting of men in a universal slavery to king, judge and priest — to the State.

Therein lies all the difference. There are struggles and conflicts which are destructive. And there are others which drive humanity forwards.

VI

In the course of the sixteenth century, the modern barbarians were to destroy all that civilisation of the cities of the Middle Ages. These barbarians did not succeed in annihilating it, but in halting its progress at least two or three centuries. They launched it in a different direction, in which humanity is struggling at this moment without knowing how to escape.

They subjected the individual. They deprived him of all his liberties, they expected him to forget all his unions based on free argument and free initiative. Their aim was to level the whole of society to a common submission to the master. They destroyed all ties between men, declaring that the State and the Church alone, must henceforth create union between their subjects; that the Church and the State alone have the task of watching over the industrial, commercial, judicial, artistic, emotional interests, for which men of the twelfth century were accustomed to unite directly.

And who are these barbarians? It is the State: the Triple Alliance, finally constituted, of the military chief, the Roman judge and the priest — the three constituting a mutual assurance for domination — the three, united in one power which will command in the name of the interests of society — and will crush that same society.

One naturally asks oneself, how were these new barbarians able to overcome the communes, hitherto so powerful? Where did they find the strength for conquest?

In the first place they found it in the village. Just as the communes of Ancient Greece proved unable to abolish slavery, and for that reason perished — so the communes of the Middle Ages failed to free the peasant from serfdom at the same time as the townsman.

It is true that almost everywhere, at the time of his emancipation, the townsman — himself a farming craftsman — had sought to carry the country folk with him to help him throw off the yoke. For two centuries, the townsmen in Italy, Spain and Germany were engaged in a bitter war against the feudal lords. Feats of heroism and perseverance were displayed by the burghers in that war on the castles. They bled themselves white to become masters of the castles of feudalism and to cut down the feudal forest that surrounded them.

But they only partially succeeded. War-weary, they finally made peace over the heads of the peasants. To buy peace, they handed over the peasants to the lord as long as he lived outside the territory conquered by the commune. In Italy and Germany they ended by accepting the lord as burgher, on condition that he came to live in the commune. Elsewhere they finished by sharing his dominion over the peasant. And the lord took his revenge on this 'low rabble' of the towns, whom he hated and despised, making blood flow on the streets by struggles and the practice of retaliation among noble families, which did not bring their differences before the syndics and the communal judges but settled them with the sword, in the street, driving one section of town-dwellers against another.

The lord also demoralised the commune with his favours, by intrigues, his lordly way of life and by his education received at the Court of the bishop or the king. He induced it to share his ambitions. And the burgher ended by imitating the lord. He became in his turn a lord, he too getting rich from distant commerce or from the labour of the serfs penned up in the villages.

After which, the peasant threw in his lot with the kings, the emperors, budding tsars and the popes when they set about building their kingdoms and subjecting the towns. Where the peasant did not march under their orders neither did he oppose them.

It is in the country, in a fortified castle, situated in the middle of rural communities that monarchy slowly came to be established. In the twelfth century, it existed in name only, and we know today what to think of the rogues, leaders of small bands of brigands who adorned themselves with that name; a name which in any case — as Augustin Thierry has so well observed — didn't mean very much at the time, when there were "the king (the superior, the senior) of the law courts", the "king of the nets" (among fishermen), the "king of the beggars".

Slowly, gropingly, a baron who was favourably situated in one region, and more powerful or more cunning than the others, would succeed in raising himself above his *confrères*. The Church hastened to support him. And by force, scheming, money, sword and poison if need be, one such feudal baron would grow in power at the expense of the others. But royal authority never succeeded in constituting itself in any of the free cities, which had their noisy forum, their Tarpeian Rock, or their river for the tyrants; it succeeded in the towns which had grown in the bosom of the country.

After having sought in vain to constitute this authority in Rheims, or in Laon, it was in Paris — an agglomeration of villages and boroughs surrounded by a rich countryside, which had not yet known the life of free cities; it was in Westminster, at the gates of the populous City of London; it was in the Kremlin, built in the centre of rich villages on the banks of the Moskva [river] after having failed in Suzdal and in Vladimir — but never in Novgorod, Pskov, Nuremberg, Laon or Florence — that royal authority was consolidated.

The peasants from the surroundings supplied the nascent monarchies with food, horses and men; commerce — royal and not communal in this case — added to their wealth. The Church surrounded them with its attention. It protected them, came to their aid with its wealth, invested for them in their local saint and his miracles. It surrounded with its veneration the Notre Dame of Paris or the Image of the Virgin of Iberia in Moscow. And while the civilisation of the free cities, freed from the bishops, gathered its youthful momentum, the Church worked relentlessly to reconstitute its authority through the intermediary of the nascent monarchy, surrounding with its attention, incense and money the royal cradle of the one it had finally chosen to re-establish with him and through him, its ecclesiastical authority. In Paris, Moscow, Madrid and Prague you see the Church bending over the cradle of royalty, a lighted torch in her hand, the executioner by her side.

Hard-working and tenacious, strengthened by her statist education, leaning on the man of strong will or cunning whom she would look for in no matter what class of society, made for intrigue and versed in Roman and Byzantine law — you can see her unrelentingly marching towards her ideal: the absolute Judaic king who nevertheless obeys the high priest — the secular arm at the orders of the ecclesiastical power.

In the sixteenth century, this slow labour of the two conspirators is already operating at full force. A king already dominates his rival fellow barons, and this power will soon be directed against the free cities to crush them in their turn.

Besides, the towns of the sixteenth century were no longer what they had been in the twelfth, thirteenth and fourteenth centuries.

Born of the libertarian revolution, they nevertheless lacked the courage or the strength to spread their ideas of equality to the neighbouring countryside, not even to those who had come later to settle in the city precincts, those sanctuaries of freedom, where they created the industrial crafts.

In every town one finds a distinction being drawn between the families who made the revolution of the twelfth century (simply known as 'the families') and those who came later and established themselves in the city. The old 'merchant guild' would not hear of accepting newcomers. It refused to absorb the 'young arts' into the commercial field. And from the simple steward to the city that it was in former times, when it carried out the external trade for the whole city, it became the middleman who got rich on his own account through foreign trade. It imported Oriental ostentation, it became moneylender to the city, and later joined the city lord and the priest against 'the lower orders'; or instead it looked to the nascent king for support of its right to enrichment and its commercial monopoly. Once commerce becomes personal the free city is destroyed.

Moreover, the guilds of the old trades, which at the beginning made up the city and its government, do not wish to recognise the same rights for the young guilds, established later by the new crafts. The latter have to conquer their rights by a revolution. And it is what they do everywhere. But whereas in some cities that revolution is the starting point for a renewal of all aspects of life as well as the arts (this is so clearly seen in Florence), in other cities it ends in the victory of the *popolo grasso* over the *popolo basso* — by a crushing repression with mass deportations and executions, especially when the seigneurs and priests interfere.

And need one add that the king will use as a pretext the defence of the 'lower classes' in order to crush the 'fat classes' and to subjugate both once he has become master of the city!

And then, the cities had to die, since *even men's ideas had changed*. The teaching of canonic law and Roman law had modified people's way of thinking.

The twelfth century European was fundamentally a federalist. As a man of free enterprise, and of free understanding, of **associations** which were freely sought and agreed to, he saw in himself the point of departure for the whole of society. He did not seek safety through obedience nor did he ask for a saviour for society. The idea of Christian and Roman discipline was unknown to him.

But under the influence of the Christian church — always in love with authority, always anxious to be the one to impose its dominion over the souls, and above all the work of the faithful; and on the other hand, under the influence of Roman law which by the twelfth century had already appeared at the courts of the powerful lords, the kings and the popes, and soon became the favourite subject at the universities — under the influence of these two teachings which are so much in accord even though originally they were bitter enemies, minds became corrupted as the priest and the legislator took over.

Man fell in love with authority. If a revolution of the lower trades took place in a commune, the commune would call for a saviour, thus saddling itself with a dictator, a municipal Caesar; it would grant him full powers to exterminate the opposition party. And he took advantage of the situation, using all the refinements in cruelty suggested to him by the Church or those borrowed from the despotic kingdoms of the Orient.

He would no doubt have the support of the Church. Had she not always dreamed of the biblical king who will kneel before the high priest and be his docile instrument? Has she not always hated with all her force those rationalist ideas which breathed in the free towns at the time of the first Renaissance, that of the twelfth century? Did she not lay her curse on those 'pagan' ideas which brought man back to nature under the influence of the rediscovery of Greek civilisation? And later did she not get the princes to stifle these ideas which, in the name of primitive Christianity, raised up men against the pope, the priest and religion in general? Fire, the wheel and the gibbet — those weapons so dear at all times to the Church — were used to crush the heretics. No matter what the instrument might be: pope, king or dictator, so long as fire, the wheel and the gibbet operated against her enemies.

And in the shadow of this double indoctrination, of the Roman jurist and the priest, the federalist spirit which had created the free commune, the spirit of initiative and free association was dying out and making way for the spirit of discipline, and pyramidal authoritarian organisation. Both the rich and the poor were asking for a saviour.

And when the saviour appeared; when the king, enriched far from the turmoil of the forum in some town of his creation, propped up by the inordinately wealthy Church and followed by defeated nobles and by their peasants, knocked at the gates of the city, promising the 'lower classes' royal protection against the rich and to the submissive rich his protection against the rebellious poor — the towns, already undermined by the cancer of authority, lacked the strength to resist him.

The great invasions of Europe by waves of peoples who had come once more from the East, assisted the rising royalty in this work of concentration of powers.

The Mongols had conquered and devastated Eastern Europe in the thirteenth century, and soon an empire was founded there, in Moscow, under the protection of the khans of Tartary and the Russian Christian Church. The Turks had come to impose themselves in Europe and pushed forward as far as Vienna, destroying everything in their way. As a result a number of powerful States were created in Poland, Bohemia, Hungary and in Central Europe to resist these two invasions. Meanwhile at the other extremity, the war of extermination waged against the Moors in Spain allowed another powerful empire to be created in Castille and Aragon, supported by the Roman Church and the Inquisition — by the sword and the stake.

These invasions and wars inevitably led Europe to enter a new phase — that of military states.

Since the communes themselves were becoming minor States, these were bound in due course to be swallowed up by the large ones.

VII

The victory of the State over the communes of the Middle Ages and the federalist institutions of the time was nevertheless not sudden. There was a period when it was sufficiently threatened for the outcome to be in doubt.

A vast popular movement — religious in its form and expressions but eminently equalitarian and communist in its aspirations — emerged in the towns and countryside of Central Europe.

Already, in the fourteenth century (in 1358 in France and in 1381 in England) two similar movements had come into being. The two powerful uprisings of the Jaquerie and of Wat Tyler had shaken society to its very foundations. Both however had been principally directed against the nobility, and though both had been defeated, they had broken feudal power. The uprising of peasants in England had put an end to serfdom and the Jaquerie in France had so severely checked serfdom in its development that from then on the institution simply vegetated, without ever reaching the power that it was to achieve later in Germany and throughout Eastern Europe.

Now, in the sixteenth century, a similar movement appeared in Central Europe. Under the name of the Hussite uprising in Bohemia, Anabaptism in Germany, Switzerland and in the Low Countries, it was — apart from the revolt against the Lords — a complete uprising against the State and Church, against Roman and canon law, in the name of primitive Christianity.[3]

For a long time misrepresented by Statist and ecclesiastical historians, this movement is only beginning to be understood today.

The absolute freedom of the individual, who must only obey the commands of his conscience, and communism were the watchwords of this uprising. And it was only later once the State and Church had succeeded in exterminating its most ardent defenders and directing it to their own ends, that this movement

---

[3]The time of troubles in Russia at the beginning of the seventeenth century, represent a similar movement, directed against serfdom and the State but without a religious basis.

reduced in importance and deprived of its revolutionary character, became the Lutherian Reformation.

With Luther the movement was welcomed by the princes; but it had begun as communist anarchism, advocated and put into practice in some places. And if one looks beyond the religious phraseology which was a tribute to the times, one finds in it the very essence of the current of ideas which we represent today: the negation of laws made by the State or said to be divinely inspired, the individual conscience being the one and only law; the commune, absolute master of its destiny, taking back from the Lords the communal lands and refusing to pay dues in kind or in money to the State; in other words communism and equality put into practice. Thus when Denck, one of the philosophers of the Anabaptist movement, was asked whether nevertheless he recognised the authority of the Bible, he replied that the only rule of conduct which each individual finds **for himself** in the Bible, was obligatory for him. And meanwhile, such vague formulas — derived from ecclesiastical jargon — that authority of 'the book' from which one so easily borrows arguments for and against communism, for and against authority, and so indefinite when it is a question of clearly affirming freedom — did not this religious tendency alone contain the germ for the certain defeat of the uprising?

Born in the towns, the movement soon spread to the countryside. The peasants refused to obey anybody and fixing an old shoe on a pike in the manner of a flag they would go about recovering the land from the lords, breaking the bonds of serfdom, driving away priest and judge, and forming themselves into free communes. And it was only by the stake, the wheel and the gibbet, by the massacre of a hundred thousand peasants in a few years, that royal or imperial power, allied to that of papal or Reformed Church — Luther encouraging the massacre of the peasants with more virulence than the pope — that put an end to those uprisings which had for a period threatened the consolidation of the nascent States.

Lutherian Reform which had sprung from popular Anabaptism, was supported by the State, massacred the people and crushed the movement from which it had drawn its strength in the beginning. Then, the remnants of the popular wave sought refuge in the communities of the 'Moravian Brothers', who in their turn were destroyed a century later by the Church and the State. Those among them who were not exterminated went to seek sanctuary, some in South Eastern Russia (the Mennonite community since emigrated to Canada), some to Greenland where they have managed ever since to live in communities and refusing all service to the State.

Henceforth the State was assured of its existence. The jurist, the priest and the war lord, joined in an alliance around the thrones, were able to pursue their work of annihilation.

How many lies have been accumulated by Statist historians, in the pay of the State, on that period!

Indeed have we not all learned at school for instance that the State had performed the great service of creating, out of the ruins of feudal society, national unions which had previously been made impossible by the rivalries between cities? Having learned this at school, almost all of us have gone on believing this to be true in adulthood.

And yet, now we learn that in spite of all the rivalries, mediaeval cities had already worked for four centuries toward building those unions, through federation, freely consented, and that they had succeeded.

For instance, the union of Lombardy, comprised the cities of Northern Italy with its federal treasury in Milan. Other federations such as the union of Tuscany, the union of Rhineland (which comprised sixty towns), the federations of Westphalia, of Bohemia, of Serbia, Poland and of Russian towns, covered Europe. At the same time, the commercial union of the Hanse included Scandinavian, German, Polish and Russian towns in all the Baltic basin. There were already all the elements, as well as the fact itself, of large groupings freely constituted.

Do you require the living proof of these groupings? You have it in Switzerland! There, the union first asserted itself among the village communes (the old cantons), just as at the same time in France it was constituted in the Laonnais. And since in Switzerland the separation between town and village had not been as far-reaching as in the countries where the towns were engaged in large-scale commerce with distant parts, the towns gave assistance to the peasant insurrection of the sixteenth century and thus the union included towns and villages to constitute a federation which continues to this day.

But the State, by its very nature, cannot tolerate a free federation: it represents that bogie of all jurists, 'a State within the State'. The State cannot recognise a freely-formed union operating within itself; it only recognises *subjects*. The State and its sister the Church arrogate to themselves alone the right to serve as the link between men.

Consequently, the State must, perforce, wipe out cities based on the direct union between citizens. It must abolish all unions within the city, as well as the city itself, and wipe out all direct union between the cities. For the federal principle it must substitute the principle of submission and discipline. Such is the stuff of the State, for without this principle it ceases to be State.

And the sixteenth century — a century of carnage and wars — can be summed up quite simply by this struggle of the nascent State against the free towns and their federations. The towns were besieged, stormed, and sacked, their inhabitants decimated or deported.

The State in the end wins total victory. And these are the consequences:

In the sixteenth century Europe was covered with rich cities, whose artisans, masons, weavers and engravers produced marvellous works of art; their universities established the foundations of modern empirical science, their caravans covered the continents, their vessels ploughed the seas and rivers.

What remained two centuries later? Towns with anything from 50,000 to 100,000 inhabitants and which (as was the case of Florence) had a greater proportion of schools and, in the communal hospitals, beds, in relation to the population than is the case with the most favoured towns today, became rotten boroughs. Their populations were decimated or deported, the State and Church took over their wealth. Industry was dying out under the rigorous control of the State's employees; commerce dead. Even the roads which had hitherto linked these cities became impassable in the seventeenth century.

State is synonymous with war. Wars devastated Europe and

managed to finish off the towns which the State had not yet directly destroyed.

With the towns crushed, at least the villages gained something from the concentration of State power? Of course not! One has only to read what the historians tell us of life in the Scottish countryside, or in Tuscany and in Germany in the sixteenth century and compare these accounts with those of extreme poverty in England in the years around 1648, in France under Louis XIV — the 'Roi Soleil' — in Germany, in Italy, everywhere, after a century of State domination.

Historians are unanimous in declaring that extreme poverty exists everywhere. In those places where serfdom had been abolished, it is reconstituted under a thousand new guises; and where it had not yet been destroyed, it emerges under the aegis of the State, as a fierce institution, displaying all the characteristics of ancient slavery or worse. In Russia it was the nascent State of the Romanovs that introduced serfdom and soon gave it the characteristics of slavery.

But could anything else come out of Statal wretchedness since its first concern, once the towns had been crushed, was to destroy the village commune and all the ties between the peasants, and then to surrender their lands to sacking by the rich and to bring them all individually into subjection to the official, the priest or the lord?

VIII

The role of the nascent State in the sixteenth and seventeenth centuries in relation to the urban centres was to destroy the independence of the cities; to pillage the rich guilds of merchants and artisans; to concentrate in its hands the external commerce of the cities and ruin it; to lay hands on the internal administration of the guilds and subject internal commerce as well as all manufactures, in every detail to the control of a host of officials — and in this way to kill industry and the arts; by taking over the local militias and the whole municipal administration, crushing the weak in the interest of the strong by taxation, and ruining the countries by wars.

Obviously the same tactic was applied to the villages and the peasants. Once the State felt strong enough it eagerly set about destroying the village commune, ruining the peasants in its clutches and plundering the common lands.

Historians and economists in the pay of the State teach us, of course, that the village commune having become an outdated form of land possession — which hampered progress in agriculture — had to disappear under 'the action of natural economic forces'. The politicians and the bourgeois economists are still saying the same thing now; and there are even some revolutionaries and socialists who claim to be scientific socialists who repeat this stock fable learned at school.

Well, never has such an odious lie been uttered in the name of science. A calculated lie since history abounds with documents to prove for those who want to know — and for France it would simply suffice to consult Dalloz — that in the first place the State deprived the village commune of all its powers: its independence, its juridical and legislative powers; and that afterwards its lands were either simply stolen by the rich with the connivance of the State, or confiscated by the State directly.

In France the pillage started in the sixteenth century, and followed its course at a greater pace in the following century. From 1659 the State started taking the communes under its wing, and one has only to refer to Louis XIV's edict of 1667, to appreciate on what

44

a scale communal goods were already being pillaged during that period. "Each one has made the best of it for his best interests...they have been shared...to fleece the communes one made use of fictitious debts," the 'Roi Soleil' said in that edict...and two years later he confiscated all the communes' income to his own advantage. Such is the meaning of 'a natural death' in the language which claims to be scientific.

In the following century, at a low estimate, half the communally-owned lands were simply taken over by the nobility and the clergy under the aegis of the State. And nevertheless the commune continued in existence until 1787. The village assembly met under the elm tree, apportioned the lands, distributed the tax demands — documentary evidence can be found in Babeau (*Le village sous l'ancien regime*). Turgot, in the province in which he was the administrator, had already found the village assemblies 'too noisy', and under his administration they were abolished and replaced by assemblies elected from among the village big-wigs. And on the eve of the Revolution of 1787, the State generalised that measure. The *mir* had been abolished, and the affairs of the commune thus came into the hands of a few syndics, elected by the richest bourgeois and peasants.

The Constituent Assembly lost no time in confirming this law in December 1789, and the bourgeois took the place of the lords to divest the communes of what communal lands remained to them. It therefore needed one Jacquerie after another in 1793 to confirm what the peasants in revolt had just achieved in Eastern France. That is to say the Constituent Assembly gave orders for the return of the communal lands to the peasants — which was in fact only done when *already achieved by revolutionary action*. It is the fate of all revolutionary laws, and it is time that it was understood. They are only enacted after the *fait accompli*.

But whilst recognising the right of the communes to the lands that had been taken away from them since 1669, the law had to add some of its bourgeois venom. Its intention was that the communal lands should be shared in equal parts only among the 'citizens' — that is among the village bourgeoisie. By a stroke of the pen it wanted to dispossess the 'inhabitants' and the bulk of the impoverished peasants, who were most in need of these lands.

Whereupon, fortunately, there were new Jacqueries and in July 1793 the convention authorised the distribution of the land among all the inhabitants individually — again something that was carried out only here and there, and served as a pretext for a new pillage of communal lands.

Were these measures not already enough to provoke what those gentlemen call 'the natural death' of the commune? yet for all that the commune went on living. So on August 24, 1794, reaction having seized power, it struck the major blow. The State confiscated all the communal lands and used them as a guarantee fund for the National Debt, putting them up for auction and surrendering them to its creatures, the Thermidorians.

This law was happily repealed on the 2 Prairial, Year V, after three years of rushing after the spoils. But by the same stroke of the pen the communes were abolished and replaced by cantonal councils, in order that the State could the more easily pack them with its creatures. This lasted until 1801 when the village communes were reintroduced; but then the Government itself undertook to appoint the mayors and syndics in each of the 36,000 communes! And this absurdity lasted until the Revolution of July 1830, after which the law of 1789 was reintroduced. And in the meantime, the communal lands were again confiscated entirely by the State in 1813 and pillaged for the next three years. What remained was not returned to the communes until 1816.

Do you think that was the end? Not at all! Each new regime saw in the communal lands a means of compensating its henchmen. Thus from 1830, on three different occasions — the first in 1837 and the last under Napoleon III — laws were promulgated to *force* the peasants to share what remained to them of the communal forests and pastures, and three times was the State obliged to abrogate these laws because of the resistance of the peasants. Nevertheless, Napoleon III took advantage of this situation to seize a few large estates and to make presents of them to his creatures.

Such are the facts. And this is what those gentlemen call in 'scientific' language the natural death of communal ownership 'under the influence of economic laws'. One might as well call the massacre of a hundred thousand soldiers on the battlefield natural death!

Now, what was done in France was also done in Belgium, in England, Germany and in Austria — everywhere in Europe except in the Slav countries.[4]

But then, the periods of outbreaks of pillaging of the communes are linked throughout Europe. Only the methods vary. Thus in England, they dared not proceed with general measures; but preferred to pass through Parliament some thousands of separate Enclosure Acts by which, in every special case, Parliament sanctioned confiscation — *it does so to this day* — and gave the squire the right to keep the communal lands that he had ring-fenced. And whereas nature had until now respected the narrow furrows by which the communal fields were divided temporarily among the families of a village in England, and though we have in the writings of somebody called Marshal clear descriptions of this form of possession at the beginning of the nineteenth century, and though communal economy has survived in some communes,[5] up to the present time, there is no lack of scholars (such as Seebohm, worthy emulator of Fustel de Coulanges) to maintain and teach that the commune never existed in England except in the form of serfdom!

In Belgium, in Germany, in Italy and Spain we find the same methods being used. And in one way or another the individual seizure of the lands that were once communal was almost completed in Western Europe by the 1850s. Of their communal lands the peasants only retain a few scraps.

This is the way the mutual alliance between the lord, the priest, the soldier and the judge, that we call the 'State', acted towards the peasants, in order to strip them of their last guarantee against extreme poverty and economic bondage.

But while the State was condoning and organising this pillage,

---

[4]It is already being done in Russia, the government having authorised the pillaging of communal lands under the law of 1906 and favoured this pillage by its own functionaries.

[5]See Dr. Gilbert Slater 'The Inclosure of Common Fields' in the *Geographical Journal of the Geographical Society of London*, with plans and maps, January 1907. Later published in volume form.

could it respect the institution of the commune as the organ of local affairs? Obviously, it could not. For to admit that some citizens should constitute a federation which takes over some of the functions of the State would have been a contradiction of first principles. The State demands from its subjects a direct, personal submission without intermediaries; it demands equality in slavery; it cannot admit of a 'State within a State'.

Thus as soon as the State began to be constituted in the sixteenth century, it sought to destroy all the links which existed among the citizens both in the towns and in the villages. Where it tolerated, under the name of municipal institutions, some remnants of autonomy — never of independence — it was only for fiscal reasons, to reduce correspondingly the central budget; or also to give the bigwigs of the province a chance to get rich at the expense of the people, as was the case in England, quite legally until recent years, and to this day in its institutions and customs.

This is understandable. Local affairs are a matter of customary law whereas the centralisation of powers is a matter of Roman law. The two cannot live side by side; the latter had to destroy the former.

It is for this reason that under the French regime in Algeria when a *kabyle djemmah* — a village commune — wants to plead for its lands, each inhabitant of the commune must lodge a personal complaint with the tribunals who will deal with fifty or two hundred isolated cases rather than accept the commune's collective plea. The Jacobin code developed in the Code Napoleon hardly recognises customary law, preferring Roman law or rather Byzantine law.

It is for this reason, again in France, that when the wind blows down a tree onto the national highway, or a peasant whose turn it is to repair the communal lane prefers to pay two or three francs to a stone breaker to do it — from twelve to fifteen employees of the Ministries of the Interior and of Finance have to be involved *and more than fifty documents* passed between these austere functionaries, before the tree can be sold, or before the peasant can receive permission to hand over his two or three francs to the communal treasury.

Those who may have doubts as to the veracity of this statement will find these fifty documents listed and duly numbered by M. Tricoche in the *Journal des Economistes* (April 1893).

That was of course under the Third Republic, for I am not talking about the barbaric procedure of the 'ancien regime' which was satisfied with five or at the most six documents. But the scholars will tell you that in more barbaric days, the control by the State was a sham.

And were it only paper work! It would only mean, after all, 20,000 officials too many, and another billion added to the budget. A mere trifle for the lovers of 'order' and alignment!

But at the bottom of all this is something much worse. There is the *principle* that destroys everything.

Peasants in a village have a large number of interests in common: household interests, neighbourhood, constant relationships. They are inevitably led to come together for a thousand different things. But the State does not want this, nor can it allow them to join together! After all the State gives them the school and the priest, the gendarme and the judge — this should be sufficient. And if other interests arise they can be dealt with through the usual channels of State and Church!

Thus until 1883 villagers in France were strictly prohibited from combining be it only for the purpose of bulk-buying of chemical fertilisers or the irrigation of their meadows. It was not until 1883-1886 that the Republic made up its mind to grant the peasants this right, by voting in the law on trades unions which however was hedged in with provisos and conditions.

And we who are stupefied by State education can rejoice in the sudden advances made by agricultural unions, without blushing at the thought that this right which has been denied the peasants until now, was one enjoyed without question by every man — free or serf — in the Middle Ages. We have become such slaves that we already look upon it as a 'victory for democracy'. This is the stage we have reached in brainwashing thanks to a system of education deformed and vitiated by the State, and our Statist prejudices!

IX

"If in the town and the village you have common interests, then ask the State or the church to deal with them. but for you to get together to deal with these interests is forbidden." This is the formula that echoes throughout Europe from the sixteenth century onwards.

Already at the end of the fourteenth century an edict by Edward III, King of England, stated that "every alliance, connivance, gatherings, meetings, enactments and solemn oaths made or to be made between carpenters and masons, are null and void". But it was only after the defeat of the villages and of the popular uprisings, to which we have already referred, that the State dared to interfere with all the institutions — guilds, brotherhoods, etc. — which bound the artisans together, to disband and destroy them.
This is what one sees so clearly in England since the vast documentation available allows one to follow this movement step by step. Little by little the State takes over all the guilds and brotherhoods. It besets them, abolishes their conjurations, their syndics, which they replace by their officers, their tribunals and their banquets; and at the beginning of the sixteenth century under Henry VIII, the State simply confiscates all that the guilds possess without bothering with formalities or procedure. The heir of the protestant king completes his task.

It is daylight robbery, without apologies as Thorold Rogers so well put it. And again, it is this theft that the so-called scientific economists describe as the 'natural' death of the guilds under the influence of 'economic laws'!

Indeed, could the State tolerate the guild, the trade corporation, with its tribunal, its militia, its treasury, its sworn organisation? It was 'the State within the State'! The real State *had* to destroy it and this it did everywhere: in England, in France, in Germany, Bohemia and Russia, maintaining only the pretence for the sake of the tax collector and as part of its huge administrative machine. And surely there is no reason to be surprised that once the guilds, and guild masterships were deprived of all that hitherto had been their lives, were put under the orders of the royal officials and had simply become cogs in the machinery of administration, that by the eighteenth century they were a hindrance, an obstacle to industrial development, in spite of the fact that for four centuries before that they represented life itself. The State had destroyed them.

But the State was not satisfied with putting a spoke in the wheels of life of the sworn brotherhoods of trades which embarrassed it by placing themselves between it and its subjects. It was not satisfied with confiscating their funds and their properties. The State had to take over their functions as well as their assets.

In a city of the Middle Ages, when there was a conflict of interests within a trade or where two different guilds were in disagreement, the only recourse was to the city. They were obliged to come to an agreement, to any kind of compromise arrangement, since they were all mutually tied up with the city. And the latter never failed to assert itself, either by arbitration or at a pinch by referring the dispute to another city.

From then on, the State was the only judge. All local conflicts including insignificant disputes in small towns with only a few hundred inhabitants, accumulated in the form of documents in the offices of the king or of parliament. The English parliament was literally inundated by thousands of minor local squabbles. As a result thousands of officials were required in the capital — most of them corruptible — to read, classify, and form an opinion on all this litigation and adjudicate on the smallest details: for example how to shoe a horse, to bleach linen, to salt herrings, to make a barrel and so on *ad infinitum*, and the wave of questions went on increasing in volume!

But this was not all. In due course the State took over export trade, seeing it as a source of profit. Formerly, when a difference arose between two towns on the value of cloth that had been exported, or of the quality of wool or over the capacity of herring barrels, the towns themselves would remonstrate with each other. If the disagreement dragged on, more often than not they would invite another town to arbitrate. Alternatively a congress of the weavers or coopers guilds would be summoned to decide on an international level the quality and value of cloth and the capacity of barrels.

But henceforth it was the State in London or in Paris which

undertook to deal with these disputes. Through its officials it controlled the capacity of barrels, defined the quality of cloth, allowing for variations as well as establishing the number of threads and their thickness in the warp and the woof, and by its ordinances meddling with the smallest details in every industry.

You can guess with what results. Under such control industry in the eighteenth century was dying.

What had in fact come of Benvenuto Cellini's art under State tutelage? it had disappeared! And the architecture of those guilds of masons and carpenters whose works of art we still admire? Just observe the hideous monuments of the statist period and at one glance you will come to the conclusion that architecture was dead, to such an extent that it has not yet recovered from the blows it received at the hands of the State.

What was happening to the textiles of Bruges and the cloth from Holland? Where were these iron-smiths, so skilled in handling iron and who, in every important European village, knew how to make this ungrateful metal lend itself to transformation into the most exquisite decorations? Where were those turners, those watchmakers, those fitters who had made Nuremberg one of the glories of the Middle Ages for precision instruments? Talk about it to James Watt who two centuries later spent thirty years in vain, looking for a worker who could produce a more or less circular cylinder for his steam engine. Consequently his machine remained at the project stage for thirty years because there were no craftsmen able to construct it.

Such was the role of the State in the industrial field. All it was capable of doing was to tighten the screw for the worker, depopulate the countryside, spread misery in the towns, reduce millions of human beings to a state of starvation and impose industrial serfdom.

And it is these pitiful remains of the old guilds, these organisms which have been battered and over-taxed, these useless cogs of the administrative machine, which the ever 'scientific' economists are so ignorant as to confuse with the guilds of the Middle Ages. What the Great French Revolution swept away as harmful to industry was not the guild, nor even the trade union, but the useless and harmful cog in the machinery of State.

But what the Revolution was at pains not to sweep away was the power of the State over industry, over the factory serf.

Do you remember the discussion which took place at the Convention — at the terrible Convention — apropos of a strike? To the complaints of the strikers the Convention replied: "The State alone has the duty to watch over the interests of all citizens. By striking, you are forming a coalition, you are creating a State within the State. So — death!"

In this reply only the bourgeois nature of the Revolution has been discerned. But has it not, in fact, a much deeper significance? Does it not sum up the attitude of the State, which found its complete and logical expression in regard to society as a whole in the Jacobinism of 1793? "Have you something to complain about? Then address your complaint to the State! It alone has the mission to redress the grievances of its subjects. As for a coalition to defend yourselves — Never!" It was in this sense that the Republic called itself one and *indivisible*.

Does not the modern socialist Jacobin think in the same way? Did not the Convention express the gist of Jacobin thought with the cold logic that is typical of it?

In this answer of the Convention was summed up the attitude of all States in regard to all coalitions and all private societies, whatever their aim.

In the case of the strike, it is a fact that in Russia it is still considered a crime of high treason. In most of Germany too where Wilhelm would say to the miners: "Appeal to me; but if ever you presume to act for yourselves you will taste the swords of my soldiers".

Such is still almost always the case in France. And even in England, only after having struggled for a century by means of secret societies, by the dagger for traitors and for the masters, by explosive powders under machines (as late as 1860), by emery powder poured into grease-boxes and so on, did British workers begin to win the right to strike, and will soon have it altogether — if they don't fall into the traps already set for them by the State, in seeking to impose compulsory arbitration in return for an eight hour day.

More than a century of bitter struggles! And what misery! how many workers died in prison, were transported to Australia, were

shot or hanged, in order to win back the right to combine which —
let it be remembered once more — every man free or serf practised
freely so long as the State did not lay its heavy hand on societies.

But then, was it the workman only who was treated in this way?

Let us simply recall the struggles that the bourgeoisie had to
wage against the State to win the right to constitute itself into
commercial societies — a right which the State only began to
concede when it discovered a convenient way of creating
monopolies for the benefit of its creatures and to fill its coffers.
Think of the struggle for the right to speak, think or write other
than the way the State decrees through the Academy, the
University and the Church! Think of the struggles that have had to
be waged to this day in order to be able to teach children to read —
a right which the State possesses but does not use! Even of the
struggles to secure the right to enjoy oneself in public! Not to
mention those which should be waged in order to dare to choose
one's judge and one's laws — a thing that was in daily use in other
times — nor the struggles that will be needed before one is able to
make a bonfire of that book of infamous punishments, invented by
the spirit of the Inquisition and of the despotic empires of the
Orient known under the name of the Penal Code!

Observe next taxation — an institution originating purely with
the State — this formidable weapon used by the State, in Europe as
in the young societies of the two Americas, to keep the masses
under its heel, to favour its minions, to ruin the majority for the
benefit of the rulers and to maintain the old divisions and castes.

Then take the wars without which States can neither constitute
themselves nor maintain themselves; wars which become
disastrous, and inevitable, the moment one admits that a particular
region — simply because it is part of a State — has interests
opposed to those of its neighbours who are part of another State.
Think of past wars and of those that subjected people will have to
wage to conquer the right to breathe freely, the wars for markets,
the wars to create colonial empires. And in France we unfortunately
know only too well that every war, victorious or not, is followed by
slavery.

And finally what is even worse than all that has just been
enumerated, is the fact that the education we all receive from the
State, at school and after, has so warped our minds that the very

notion of freedom ends up by being lost, and disguised in servitude.

It is a sad sight to see those who believe themselves to be revolutionaries unleashing their hatred on the anarchist — just because his views on freedom go beyond their petty and narrow concepts of freedom learned in the State school. And meanwhile, this spectacle is a reality. The fact is that the spirit of voluntary servitude was always cleverly cultivated in the minds of the young, and still is, in order to perpetuate the subjection of the individual to the State.

Libertarian philosophy is stifled by the Roman and Catholic pseudo-philosophy of the State. History is vitiated from the very first page, where it lies when speaking of the Merovingian and Carolingian monarchies, to the last page where it glorifies Jacobinism and refuses to recognise the role of the people in creating the institutions. Natural sciences are perverted in order to be put at the service of the double idol: Church-State. Individual psychology, and even more that of societies, are falsified in each of their assertions in justifying the triple alliance of soldier, priest and judge. Finally, morality, after having preached for centuries obedience to the Church, or the book, achieves its emancipation today only to then preach servility to the State: "No direct moral obligations towards your neighbour, nor even any feeling of solidarity; all your obligations are to the State", we are told, we are taught, in this new cult of the old Roman and Caesarian divinity. "The neighbour, the comrade, the companion — forget them. You will henceforth only know them through the intermediary of some organ or other of your State. And every one of you will make a virtue out of being equally subjected to it."

And the glorification of the State and of its discipline, for which the university and the Church, the press and the political parties labour, is propagated so successfully that even revolutionaries dare not look this fetish straight in the eye.

The modern radical is a centralist. Statist and rabid Jacobin. And the socialist falls into step. Just as the Florentines at the end of the fifteenth century knew no better than to call on the dictatorship of the State to save themselves from the Patricians, so the socialists can only call upon the same Gods, the dictatorship of the State, to save themselves from the horrors of the economic regime created by that very same State!

X

If one goes a little deeper into these different categories of phenomena which I have hardly touched upon in this short outline, one will understand why — seeing the State as it has been in history, and as it is in essence today — and convinced that a social institution cannot lend itself to *all* the desired goals, since, as with every organ, it developed according to the function it performed, in a definite direction and not in all possible directions — one will understand, I say, why the conclusion we arrive at is for the abolition of the State.

We see it in the Institution, developed in the history of human societies to prevent the direct association among men to shackle the development of local and individual initiative, to crush existing liberties, to prevent their new blossoming — all this in order to subject the masses to the will of minorities.

And we know an institution which has a long past going back several thousand years cannot lend itself to a function opposed to the one for which and by which it was developed in the course of history.

To this absolutely unshakeable argument for anyone who has reflected on history, what reply do we get? One is answered with an almost childish argument:

'The State exists and represents a powerful ready-made organisation. Why not use it instead of wanting to destroy it? It operates for evil ends — agreed; but the reason is that it is in the hands of the exploiters. If it were taken over by the people, why would it not be used for better ends, for the good of the people?'

Always the same dream — that of the Marquis de Posa, in Schiller's drama seeking to make an instrument of emancipation out of absolutism; or again the dream of the gentle Abbé Pierre in Zola's *Rome* wanting to make of the Church the lever for socialism.

How sad it is to have to reply to such arguments! For those who argue in this way either haven't a clue as to the true historic role of the State, or they view the social revolution in such a superficial and painless form that it ceases to have anything in common with their socialist aspirations.

Take the concrete example of France.

All thinking people must have noticed the striking fact that the Third Republic, in spite of its republican form of government, has remained monarchist in essence. We have all reproached it for not having republicanised France — I am not saying that it has done nothing for the *social* revolution, but that it has not even introduced a morality — that is an outlook which is simply republican. For the little that has been done in the past 25 years to democratise social attitudes or to spread a little education has been done everywhere, in all the European monarchies, under pressure from the times through which we are passing. Then where does this strange anomaly of a republic which has remained a monarchy come from?

It arises from the fact that France has remained a State, and exactly where it was thirty years ago. The holders of power have changed the name but all that huge ministerial scaffolding, all that centralised organisation of white-collar workers, all this apeing of the Rome of the Caesars which has developed in France, all that huge organisation to assure and extend the exploitation of the masses in favour of a few privileged groups, which is the essence of the State institution — all that has remained. And those wheels of bureaucracy continue as in the past to exchange their fifty documents when the wind has blown down a tree on to the highway and to transfer the millions deducted from the nation to the coffers of the privileged. The official stamp on the documents has changed; but the State, its spirit, its organs, its territorial centralisation, its centralisation of functions, its favouritism, and its role as creator of monopolies have remained. Like an octopus they go on spreading their tentacles over the country.

The republicans — and I am speaking of the sincere ones — had cherished the illusion that one could 'utilise the organisation of the State' to effect a change in a Republican direction, and these are the results. Whereas it was necessary to break up the old organisation, *shatter the State* and rebuild a new organisation from the very foundations of society — the liberated village commune, federalism, groupings from simple to complex, free working association — they thought of using the 'organisation that already existed'. And, not having understood that, one does not make an historical institution follow in the direction to which one points —

that is in the opposite direction to the one it has taken over the centuries — they were swallowed up by the institution.

And this happened though in this case it was not even a question yet of changing the whole economic relations in society! The aim was merely to reform only some aspects of political relations between men.

But after such a complex failure, and in the light of such a pitiful experiment, there are those who still insist in telling us that the conquest of powers in the State, by the people, will suffice to accomplish the social revolution! — that the old machine, the old organisation, slowly developed in the course of history to crush freedom, to crush the individual, to establish oppression on a legal basis, to create monopolists, to lead minds astray by accustoming them to servitude — will lend itself perfectly to its new functions: that it will become the instrument, the framework for the germination of a new life, to found freedom and equality on economic bases, the destruction of monopolies, the awakening of society and towards the achievement of a future of freedom and equality!

What a sad and tragic mistake!

To give full scope to socialism entails rebuilding from top to bottom a society dominated by the narrow individualism of the shopkeeper. It is not as has sometimes been said by those indulging in metaphysical wooliness just a question of giving the worker 'the total product of his labour'; it is a question of completely reshaping all relationships, from those which exist today between every individual and his churchwarden or his station-master to those which exist between trades, hamlets, cities and regions. In every street, in every hamlet, in every group of men gathered around a factory or along a section of the railway line, the creative, constructive and organisational spirit must be awakened in order to rebuild life — in the factory, in the village, in the store, in production and in distribution of supplies. All relations between individuals and great centres of population have to be made all over again, from the very day, from the very moment one alters the existing commercial or administrative organisation.

And they expect this immense task, requiring the free expression of popular genius, to be carried out within the framework of the

State and the pyramidal organisation which is the essence of the State! They expect the State whose very raison d'être is the crushing of the individual, the hatred of initiative, the triumph of *one* idea which must be inevitably that of mediocrity — to become the lever for the accomplishment of this immense transformation. They want to direct the renewal of a society by means of decrees and electoral majorities...How ridiculous!

Throughout the history of our civilisation, two traditions, two opposing tendencies have confronted each other: the Roman and the Popular; the imperial and the federalist; the authoritarian and the libertarian. And this is so, once more, on the eve of the social revolution.

Between these two currents, always manifesting themselves, always at grips with each other — the popular trend and that which thirsts for political and religious domination — we have made our choice.

We seek to recapture the spirit which drove people in the twelfth century to organise themselves on the basis of free agreement and individual initiative as well as of the free federation of the interested parties. And we are quite prepared to leave the others to cling to the imperial, the Roman and canonical tradition.

History is not an uninterrupted natural development. Again and again development has stopped in one particular territory only to emerge somewhere else. Egypt, the Near East, the Mediterranean shores and Central Europe have all in turn been centres of historical development. But every time the pattern has been the same: beginning with the phase of the primitive tribe followed by the village commune; then by the free city, finally to die with the advent of the State.

In Egypt, civilisation begins with the primitive tribe. It advances to the village commune and later to the period of the free cities; later still to the State which, after a period in which it flourished, leads to death.

Development starts afresh in Syria, in Persia and in Palestine. It follows the same pattern: the tribe, the village commune, the free city, the all-powerful State and...death!

A new civilisation then comes to life in Greece. Always through the tribe. Slowly it reaches the level of the village commune and then to the republican cities. In these cities civilisation reaches its zenith. But the East communicates its poisonous breath, its traditions of despotism. Wars and conquests create the Empire of Alexander of Macedonia. The State asserts itself, grows, destroys all culture and...it is death.

Rome in its turn restarts civilisation. Once more one finds at the beginning the primitive tribe, then the village commune followed by the city. At this phase Rome was at the height of its civilisation. But then come the State and the Empire and then...death!

On the ruins of the Roman Empire, Celtic, Germanic, Slavonic and Scandanavian tribes once more take up the threads of civilisation. Slowly the primitive tribe develops its institutions and manages to build up the village commune. It lingers in this phase until the twelfth century when the republican city arises, and this brings with it the blossoming of the human spirit, proof of which are the masterpieces of architecture, the grandiose development of the arts, the discoveries which lay the foundations of natural sciences...But then the State emerges...Death? Yes: death — or renewal!

Either the State for ever, crushing individual and local life, taking over in all fields of human activity, bringing with it all its wars and domestic struggles for power, its palace revolutions which only replace one tyrant by another, and inevitably at the end of this development there is...death!

Or the destruction of States, and new life starting again in thousands of centres on the principle of the lively initiative of the individual and groups and that of free agreement.

The choice lies with you!

Peter Kropotkin
ACT FOR YOURSELVES!

This volume comprises seventeen articles by Kropotkin first published in *Freedom* in 1887-1888, but which have never been reprinted though it is on record that Kropotkin himself would have liked to see them published in book form. The FREEDOM PRESS Centenary volumes project made it essential to include these important and unknown writings by Kropotkin as a supplement to volume 1 *Freedom* (1886-1936).

The title, *Act for Yourselves!*, has been taken from one of the articles as expressing the message of the whole series, and is above all a programme of anarchist communist thought and action in the situation of Britain a century ago, which isn't so very different from that of Britain today.

The volume has been edited, annotated and introduced by Heiner Becker and Nicolas Walter.

Ready spring 1987

96 pages   ISBN 0 900384 387   £2.50

FREEDOM PRESS
1987

Peter Kropotkin
ANARCHISM
&
ANARCHIST
COMMUNISM
Edited with notes
by Nicolas Walter

Both essays have been reprinted at various times in various forms, but this is their first appearance together in properly edited versions so that they may once more provide authoritative accounts of classic anarchism for general readers. Despite the lapse of time, they will be found as interesting and instructive as ever, and they will still offer a good basic introduction to anarchist theory and history.

64 pages   ISBN 0 900384 344   £1.75

FREEDOM PRESS
1987

Peter Kropotkin
MUTUAL AID
A Factor of Evolution

Undoubtedly Kropotkin's most important and best known book, as relevant today as when it was first published in 1902.

This FREEDOM PRESS edition includes by way of an Introduction:

John Hewetson's
Mutual Aid and Social Evolution

Ready spring 1987

300 pages   ISBN 0 900384 360   £4.00

FREEDOM PRESS
1987

Peter Kropotkin
FIELDS, FACTORIES
AND WORKSHOPS
TOMORROW
Edited, Introduced and
with additional material
by Colin Ward

"The ways that Kropotkin suggested, how men can at once begin to live better, are still the ways; the evils he attacked here...still the evils."
PAUL GOODMAN

"I wish, finally, to praise the careful editing of this book...In these fascinating notes the threads of an alternative tradition in political thinking are quietly drawn together: the works of Gandhi, Buber, Paul Goodman, Herbert Read, Lewis Mumford and many others are knitted into one coherent fabric. Here is a suppressed tradition of philosophy and politics, which as Marxist and capitalist ideology disintegrate or ossify, more and more people will be wanting to consider."
PETER ABBS in *The Ecologist*

213 pages   ISBN 0 900384 263   £3.50

FREEDOM PRESS
1985